BOYS WILL BE BOYS

CALLUM HOLGATE

BOYS WILL BE BOYS

BOYS WILL BE BOYS
A COLLECTION OF POETRY

by
Callum Holgate

INTRODUCTION

Boys Will Be Boys is the product of three years of writing and just as much procrastination. As my friends and family know, I have been writing poetry for over five years but only sharing it publicly as a form of therapy for roughly two. What began as a method of computing thoughts or sharing the words I would not usually be brave enough to say out loud has evolved into my greatest passion. Poetry is a shining light in a relatively bleak time of my life.

I am not usually earnest, and those who know me well will find this introduction to be quite unlike me. However, I felt that I needed to show readers the process behind the poetry and the positive change that every reader and friend I have gained through my poetry has had on my life. Without the support of my good friends, my poetic acquaintances, my various teachers, the artists I have met online, and especially my parents, I may not have developed my passion for poetry, nor the confidence to share it. I would not be the person I am today if it weren't for the incredible support I received while sharing my silly little thoughts and observations throughout the last few years. Thank you.

With that said, I'll return to my typical, emotionally void self and ask that you please enjoy the following pages of poetry. If by the end, you didn't enjoy it, it's too late. I have already wasted your time and money, and there's no way of getting that back. Unless you refund my book. Please don't refund my book. Sorry. Please direct all complaints to my Instagram page, @CallumCanon, but make sure that you follow it and like all the posts first. That is the only way for your complaints to be registered. Again, thank you for the support, and please don't refund my book.

Callum

I

BOYS WILL BE BOYS

BOYS WILL BE BOYS

"Boys will be boys,"
my mother always said
when my brother fell
and hit his head.
But wiped away
the tear from his eye
because boys will be boys,
and boys don't cry.

Boys will be boys,
and they'll get back up,
back to their feet,
brush off the dust
from their black and white shirts,
for they never wear pink
And boys do not cry.
No, instead they drink.
Crying is for pussies—
the mark of the girl.

No, boys keep it tight
and never unfurl.
There's no room in this world
for a boy who's a girl.

Because boys will be boys.
It's clear to see.
And you'd better not be
in touch at all
with femininity.
We stamp that out
as soon as we can.
'Cause boys should be boys,
not a fucking woman

But boys will be boys,
and they will get on
when the night is cold
and the day is long.
So, put away your tissues.
Don't get it wrong.
No, boys don't cry
because they are strong.

Boys will be boys,
and they'd better not talk
because talking's weak
and boys are not.
So, when we fall,
instead we drink.

No, boys don't cry
because men don't think.

And men don't think
because men aren't real.
And men aren't real
because men can't feel.
Because boys will be boys
and they'll play outside
and they'll shave their beards
and they will not cry.
And they'll drink their beers
and they'll fuck their wives
because they're the guy
with his feet on the ground
and his head in the sky.
Because he's the man
and he never cries.

And men don't cry.
No, instead we die,
quietly and nobly,
by suicide.
We take our lives
and make no noise
because boys don't cry.
Because boys must be boys.

I HOPE THIS FINDS YOU WELL

One day, I'll write myself a poem
fit to burst with the words
I could never use to describe her.
Affirmations and confirmations
of everything I've ever wanted
to think or say
to you.

But for now, I'll write a poem
about writing myself a poem
about the thoughts
I'm not ready to have.

I'M NOT SURE WHAT TO CALL THIS ONE; PROBABLY OVERTHINKING, OR SOMETHING

Fret not, my dear.
"Overthinking" is my middle name.

Well, not really.
It's actually James,
after my dad,
who never overthinks anything
and somehow raised me
from the age of twenty.

While, at the age of twenty,
I just found out
the phrase is
"deep-seated,"
not "deep-seeded."
So, really, it's no surprise

I'm waiting for a call back
from an NHS therapy scheme.

A SONNET FOR MY YOUNGER SELF

Oh, to be a child on trampoline,
or sculpting toxic lunch from plasticine.
Drinking Capri Suns at three-fifteen,
running through the fields so young and green.
Lying on our backs, eyes to the clouds,
a single body 'mong the sports day crowds.
That future piercing scent of thick sun cream.
Those wispy summer eves, they seem a dream.
But now my hours are spent in the back,
in stocking rooms. I'm counting cans to stack,
not fruit shoots or cola icy pops
Instead, my life's consumed by watching clocks.
And thus, I search for whimsy, time to time,
but cream is never needed with no shine.

UNTITLED POEM #1

Gone, now, are the sweaty onions in the
Rain, while the screams of machines
Attacked our ears on our corner of the track.
Now silence
Deafens us.
Animosity
Destroyed us.

HARPSICHORD SOLOS FOR MEN WHO LIKE TO WEAR PINK TO FAMILY EVENTS

Listening to the tickling
of Harpsichord keys
that form the soundtrack
of the questions they'll ask,
some hidden atom bomb.
He calls curiosity
a minefield
of polite conversation,
a demonstration of introspection.

Try and find a way to tell her
some queries simply have no answer.

UNTITLED POEM #2

I wish I could see myself now,
but I tore my eyes out
in a hotel bathroom
three years ago to the day,
in a mirror that's seen
a thousand fucking faces,
all with their thumbs in their eyes.

POCKET CHANGE

You can't put a price on happiness,
but my antidepressants are £9.50.
That's thirty-one p a day.

~

Which if you ask me,
Ain't a fair price to pay.
I get just as much serotonin
from shrugging out "we move,"
and that shit's free to say.

ALIEN (1979)

One time,
when I watched Alien (1979),
that part where the Alien (1979)
puts its tendril in the man's mouth
made me feel a little funny,
like there was something inside me.

But it was no xenomorph.
No Alien (1979) was in me that day,
but I definitely felt a little something
in an Alien (1979) way.

NEW PLAYLIST

She fucks other people
to the songs you recommend.
Tugs on the jeans
of the boys who pretend
to love her.

The boys your mother warned you about.
The boys your brothers become.

Those cutting choruses
soundtrack the slice of a switchblade
snapping open in the dark,
held against skin,
raw and bloody,
to be scored and sealed
in a vacuum-packed bandage,

to scar and stagnate.
A tattoo of trauma.

BUTTERFLIES

I'm swallowing caterpillars.
Expect butterflies in my stomach
in two to five business days
because these pill bugs
that fill my gullet
have replaced blue sky with greys,
and that flutter in my belly
sadly flew away.

Now all I feel is tired.
Although, I guess I'm glad.
The realm of sleep is more desired
than barren meadows of the sad.

COMEDY OF ERRORS

My words promote my death.
A billboard for a funeral parlour.
A friendly face,
a smile across the tracks.
The demagogue writes it true.

I'd tell you that I want to die,
each day more than last,
but I told myself I'd never lie,
ne'er to dredge from sunken past.
And that is why I do not cry.
I dress my sorrow in a smile,
veil my turmoil in a laugh,
to split the black once in a while.

DOTTED GREEN LINES

One foot in front of other.
Laces tied, as taught by mother.
Avoiding cracks and dodging brother.
I learned to walk in yesteryear,
along the paves and paths and tracks,
cobbled stones or fresh tarmac.
Never I thought that I'd turn back
to wishful steps of yesteryear.
Though the hardware still remains,
and there's no damage 'tween feet and brain,
I seem to suffer placebo strain
when I come to stroll like yesteryear.
With every byway cordoned off,
every road sign 'blazened "STOP,"
breath and song for ash I'll swap.
I'll never walk like yesteryear.
No hand to hold or stroller pushed,
clutching bags, deflowering bush.
Instead, now its demons shushed
as I long to stride in yesteryear,
where bells would ring and signal ends

for eating crisps and pushing friends.
The chatter now, inside it rends.
I'm not the same as yesteryear.
Not a thought now of "I can't wait
to don the shoes and perambulate
to every meeting with every mate."
It is no longer yesteryear.
Now put them in and drown him out.
In podcasts I can bury shouts,
but eventually the songs run out,
and I'm far away from yesteryear.
I let them hang around my throat.
They've drained the water from the moat.
My headphone wire now garrotte
betwixt the 'knucks of yesteryear.
A vision comes of primary school,
the cobble out back in shade and cool,
the final thoughts of a wistful fool
who lived and died in yesteryear.

GROWING

I wish I could show you
who I'd turn out to be,
every place that I would go,
everything that I would see.

And while I cannot take you
everywhere you wished to go,
I await your presence every day,
like the first December snow.

BUBBLE WRAP

A creature lost in thought,
selling whispersilk dreams to its youth.
Dressing wounds and nightmares
in the blasphemer's cloth.
Tying bows in ribbon-rope
around caramel-scented barbs
and air-brushing fortune across
the face of a weighted die.
Wrap the Brussel sprouts in bubble gum
and force-feed the starving.
Polish their gemstone eyes
with a base of lead
so that a day in the sun
barely resembles an unmarked walnut.
She slides a sugar pill down the throat
of sickly babes,
massaging SPF 50 into a bumblebee
while installing the fourth camera
into the eyes of a porcelain doll.
Not a Kevlar vest or rape alarm in sight.
No bottle of triple-distilled spring water,

nor even a limescaleless tap,
for a country mile.
No, your poisoned youth crosses the road
from the parish chaplain,
tightening their Velcro as
the oncoming Boeing
crashes head-first
wailing, into a red-helmeted, shaven skull.

SUNGLASSES ON THE DINING TABLE

Sunglasses on the dining table,
stained and dirtied.
She cries for the man
she dreamt would save her,
save her from the fate
she would cultivate

HEADLIGHTS

Your eyes are headlights
and I am transfixed,
staring into the depths
of the haze that sits
betwixt your headlights,
beckoning me to feel
how short life can be
with my head
beneath your wheel.

What's this I see?
A deer, sweet child,
locked in the light
of my high beams,
staring into my headlights,
forgetting who they are
or what brought them here,
how it feels

with their eyes in mine
and their head
beneath my wheels.

UNTITLED POEM #3

I don't recognise

myself

in your bathroom

mirror.

A NIGHTINGALE

A nightingale sits,
perched on a frost-dusted windowsill,
opening its wings.
In doing so, sprinkling the world below
with soft powder.
A year wasted,
waiting for such a nightingale to arrive.
Luckily still, friend,
the frost-bed welcomes you in April,
for without it
you are nothing
less than a common thrush or
perhaps a robin.
Yet, here a nightingale sits,
perched on frost.
Open your mouth,
sweet nightingale, and fill the air
with all you have.

UNTITLED POEM #4

Cheap drinks and love bites—
you can be a queen for the night,
but with the morning sun
your face becomes
a spectre of the one I loved
when I was fifteen.

ALONE

There's a hundred different versions of me.
One probably knows what he wants;
another, what he needs.
Somewhere, there's a version of me
content with himself,
holding a hand stronger than his.

One of them is God,
even just for a moment.
He creates
while the other ninety-nine destroy.

There's a hundred different versions of me,
and each one sits alone,
his only friend
the pen.

UNTITLED POEM #5

Putting toys at the bottom of cereal
is a dangerous precedent for kids
'cause I've made it to the bottom
of countless bottles of rum,
and all I've ever found
is myself,
alone.

A COUNSELLOR'S INCUBATION

Months have passed since I told you that lie,
planted a faint kiss on your forehead crease,
and left the car, tail between my legs
and a mind in tatters.

All that is with me now, just know,
sealed nicely in the bouncing of a leg
or the tremble of a coffee cup
clasped in sweating palms.

Mother told me to do this.
I'd only joked, read articles,
put my name down on the site,
exchanged emails with the support team,
showered this morning,
and left early to get here on time.

~

You'd laugh to see me now,
opposite her; leg still bouncing
and a mouth dryer than our correspondence.
"Good for you," you'd say.

~

Well, yes, actually.

~

Good for me.
For this emperor has shed his tattered rags,
and donned new clothes,
painting eyes on moth wings,
and leaving her chrysalis a butterfly.
Or, at least, a caterpillar.

II

WORDS FOR THE ONES THAT DON'T EXIST

WORDS FOR THE ONES THAT DON'T EXIST

I do not exist,
nor have I existed
since the day I sold my heart
to this page,
opened up my veins
and bled 'til the white washed away.

There are others
reading between the lines.
Their pillows carve into their cheeks
at two in the afternoon
on a weekday,
bedridden and broken,
with sullied carpets
messier than their heads.

We do not exist,

but rather we are here,
present but vacant,
drifting through the tide
of a world that wasn't for us.

~

There are no words
for the ones that don't exist.
No soothing songs
to ease the clamour
of a vapid planet.
No music to soundtrack
the violence of silence.

~

The ones that don't exist
live in the gaps between
reality and realism,
between what they have created
and what they do not allow us to see.

~

I do not exist.
My words exist.

~

The words for the ones that don't exist
are the ones they choose to write.

WHAT WE OWE TO EACH OTHER

Thank you.

~

I begin things as I mean to go on,
with your signature on my cast
and two words I promised to write.

~

Thank you.

POGO STICK

I often feel like a pogo stick:
absolutely useless
three hundred and sixty-four days a year.
But at least a bit of fun
the day you remember that I'm here.

SCRATCH CARDS

Empty scratch cards on the pavement
of the shit neighbourhoods,
a sickening reminder
of what could've been,
a scratch-and-sniff whiff
of a better life
they want to live.

Discard the card;
collect the dole
with dust under your fingernails.

ROBIN

I was walking home
when I saw a tiny bird—
a robin,
I think.
It had a red belly.

I thought to myself,
"I could crush this bird
in my hands
if it trusts me
enough to let me."

I kept walking home
without looking up.

ATTENTION DEFICIT

Do you recall when my leg would bounce
to the beat of our racing hearts?
When a laugh is exchanged
across a room
at the expense of a serpent's words,
we are united by our
mutual love
for a demonic masquerade
and a sorrowful addition to a bowl
of pre-work self-reflection.
I recall all too well.
And when recollection is washed
with a dirtied rag
and dried with a bloodied tissue,
wrought from the nosebleeds
suffered in pursuit of a giggle,
I can only wonder
what might have been
had my leg had two racings hearts
whose beat it could imitate.

A ONE-SIDED CONVERSATION WITH A LOOKING GLASS

Red just isn't you—
and Christ, that's too revealing.
Surely, there's something you fit into
that's a tad bit more appealing.

Your tits look flat. Your hair's a mess.
You're far too fat to wear that dress.
Your skin's not clear, so I think, my dear,
we'll just stay in tonight.

Clean off your face.
What a disgrace.
Who'd ever love you anyway?
If not yourself,
then no one else.

I'll try again another day.

UNTITLED POEM #6

I once spoke to a frog
with orange and purple markings,
which Mum had warned me not to do.
He leapt from leaf to frond
while his cousin in the garden pond
decorated a Facebook page.
His eyes, all wide and red,
while you upon the hand of man
render man soon dead.

That's when my venomed friend
croaked out words that coat my head:
"I leap from leaf to frond,"
he said,
"because I mean man no harm.
Man begets death to man
when he takes me in his arms,
to place me upon the plastic leaf
where there's no juices in the fronds,

while he flashes fancy camera lights
at my cousin in the pond."

≈

"But my friend," I retort,
"there's poison in your bones.
Though you are small,
your skin is made to kill a man.
How can you be glad at all?"

≈

"You see, my child," he ribbits back,
"there's defence in what you call
my great offence to humankind.
Though we're not the same at all,
the frog is but a speckled man.
There's a poison in us all."

BILLS BILLS BILLS BILLS BILLS

Do what you are told to do.
Go to college.
Get a degree.
Find a job.
Work for me.
Save your money; do not spend it
because the times ahead are dangerous.
Though, I will bleed your pockets dry
and with it become infamous.
What's yours is mine.
What's mine expands.
That is the only answer.
So, place your health into my hands.
My balance swells; I am your cancer.

UNTITLED POEM #7

I'm staring blankly out of windows
that lead to nowhere,
into reflections of faces
I do not recognise,
nor wish to know,
into bleak fields of dying roses
where nothing new will grow,
where the living go to die
and the dead go to live.

I'm boarding up the windows
with empty cardboard boxes,
obscuring the man on the other side
who tends to the wilting flowers
and collects the petals to crush
down to a fine powder
to be mixed
and drunk.

THIS IS NOT A POEM

This is not a poem.
It's a cry for help,
an endless scream into an endless void.

Because I am not a poet.
In fact, I'm barely a man,
too scared to wake, too nervous to sleep.

This is not a poem.
This is a confession
etched in notepad paper
and written in blood.

This is not
a poem.

～

this
is
not
a
poem.

ONE TEASPOON OF SUGAR

A face for every bubble in the foam of a coffee-shop latte

and a smile for, perhaps, no more than a third.

More of these faces, disembodied from their lives,

tend more so to scowl at this window,

either at the realm that lives behind it,

or the one reflected within.

That's why you precious few,

those who return my mouth-corner call,

are immortalised here,

sharing with a tally mark

a gift given for free

and opened with no real reaction

or value,

but rather a contract

between two souls,

simultaneously signed

and repealed,

for us to go about

our scowling days again.

STRANGERS

there's truly no difference
between x or y

the story so far
was written by those
with an agenda
the ones who'd never
even think to extend
a palm in the dark
to pluck you up
from out of this

we strangers stay estranged
until the moments that we kiss

THAT'S HOW YOU BE ME

Clashing sounds of crashing hands,
tickling ivories with the grace of
every bull in every china shop.

She stumbles through each note of "Greensleeves,"
just like Mum,
heeding every word before casting them aside.
Guidance is the net in a sea of youthful genius.

Follow this fleeting passion
before she runs away
along the carpal tunnel
and the aged self-doubt.
Embrace this aural lover;
hold her hand and sing with her into the night
before that remorseless scythe of responsibility
seeks to reap your innocence,

and with it, harvest ripening potential.

～

Spit in the face of the prosecutor
and never bow to any oppressor,
for your music is sweeter than birdsong
and more powerful than the boulder
with which he wills to block your passage.

～

Take his cries, his dismissal,
and with it whet your blade.
Fire back a barbed bolt of belief
and split the silence.

～

Let every fingertip coerce our understanding
of song, of sound, and of you.
Every scale carries your voice,
and each semi-quaver resonates your message.

～

"That's how you be me."

UNTITLED POEM #8

When I pass on,
pass on a thousand roses
to my grave,
one for every colour
in every spectrum,
each one left with
each one of its thorns.

(ON THE ACT OF SCREAMING INTO)
MIRRORS

I have gone from
screaming from the rooftops—
shouting from the sky
the colours of the rainbow
the apple of my eye—
to screaming in the mirror,
shouting to my mind,
where the only one who listens
is the man behind the eyes
who wraps his rope
around my throat
and sticks his nails into my thighs.

So, I shout
and shout again
in the darkness of it all.
I shout
with a mouth
stitched shut

and bloody raw.

The mirror never ends.
It just spits back the words I give.
I will never make amends.
I will never outlive
the man who holds the dagger,
runs its blade across my skin.
The man whose grip is on my lungs
saps the air and makes it thin.

My words are close to worthless
to the mirror in the hall,
but I will not stop shouting
in the darkness of it all.

FOXES

I've seen so many foxes tonight,
orange and white
and afraid
of the light from the car.

I don't know who
or what
might have sent them my way,
nor whether I'm supposed to
gain something
from their visit.
Or are they just
foxes?

I hope they're not just foxes.

LET ME SLEEP

Let me sleep for evermore,
for my tongue, it bleeds.
My eyes are sore.
I cannot bear wake anymore.
Let me sleep for evermore.

Let me dream forever now,
for my mind, it's sleeping.
I know not how
I will avoid that sombre bough.
Let me dream forever now.

Let me rest forever, please,
for my lungs are empty.
I simply wheeze.
Fill them up with dream's soft breeze.
Let me rest forever, please.

~

Let me live forever there,
for my heart, it yearns
yet seldom cares
for everything we'd ever share.
Let me live forever there.

~

Let me die, forever sleep,
for my dreams sow seeds
I'll never reap.
There she stands, though she does not weep.
Please if not death, simply sleep,
for my reality does not seep
'twixt the seams of slumbers deep,
'neath the lochs and vales miskeep'd,
nor into dreams
or into sleep.
There you stand,
and there I'll keep
the crops I swore
I'd never reap.
Reality's dreams
manifest in sleep.

~

Alas, each day, I surely wake.
Morning's cruel claws surely take
all those dreams I sought to make.
Daring to dream, my sole mistake.

WAVES

I put my ear to a conch shell
fifteen miles from the nearest ocean,
but all I heard was the screeching
of those tortured tires.

Not even closing my eyes
nor cutting out my tongue
could accentuate her waves.

Somewhere, in a conch shell
homed on a mantlepiece,
is a piece of you.

UNTITLED POEM #9

Flowers have lost their colour.
Bees have lost their stripes.
You've poisoned yet another,
poured your venom in the pipes.
You've lost sight of what is true,
what means anything at all.
You have lost what makes you you.
You're preparing for a fall
the scale of which you've never seen,
nor hoped to know.
You don't know what you really mean.
You don't know where to go.
The trees have lost their leaves again.
The sun has lost its shine.
There's a sickness on the breeze again.
The clocks have lost their time.
You're sure there's only darkness left,
just one road your head can take.
The ribbon that once held you's cleft.
There's a decision you should make.
Break the glass and ring the fire bell.

Call the number on your wrist,
or push the knife in further still
and give it a wicked twist.
Write a letter to the man in white,
tell him what ails your soul,
or step upon the marble stairs
and become a speck amidst the mould.

THERE'S A CLOCK ON THE WALL

There's a clock on the wall
of the room I'm in tonight,
constantly ticking
and ticking,
ticking
every second
as clocks do.
And with each tick,
it makes its way back into my head.

Don't think about the ticking.
Ignore the ticking.
Forget there ever was a clock
on the wall of the room
I'm in tonight,
constantly ticking.
But I can't.
With each tick,
I'm reminded of the last,

reminded there will be another.

~

So, I make noise
to drown out the ticking
of the clock on the wall
of the room I'm in tonight.
But the ticking still remains
in the centre of it all,
louder than the rustling of bedsheets
or the slow, rhythmic rise
and fall
of my chest.
The ticking never stops.

~

Because I'll never get up
I'll never take the batteries out
I'll never put the clock in another room
There will forever be
a clock on the wall
of the room I'm in tonight
constantly ticking
and ticking
Ticking
and ticking
Ticking
and ticking
and ticking
and ticking
and ticking

But I've done it now.
I did get up.
I did put the clock in another room,
and now it's gone.
The ticking
and the ticking
and the ticking
is in another room,
one without me.
And it has left a space,
left its mark,
left its ticking
etched forever in my brain
and louder now
in the silence of it all.

There is no clock on the wall
of the room I'm in tonight,
just the hanger
that held it
and allowed it to tick.

UNTITLED POEM #10

I want to get off the train,
hop off halfway
to my end point.

I want to visit you
in fields of flowers
under an unknown sun.

ON LEAVES

Rainwater flows past my feet,
a dirty inner-city river.
I think myself a leaf
so that it might deliver
me to some other place,
a refuse gutter reservoir.
You'd call me a disgrace
in this precipitation abattoir.

The only sin is sentience
among the fag butts and the filth.
Tear away at my intelligence.
And all the better still,
pluck apart my features, let my body lapse
into a leaf, sans skin and bone.
Lay me amidst the crumbs and scraps
on my crisp packet throne.

Break me from the bough.
Let me drift in swift canals
cutting through this pavement.
I'm more alive somehow
than I'd ever be as me.
I leave this world a boy
to drown among the leaves.

UNTITLED POEM #11

Tie me up in Leavers hoodies.
Kiss me into napkins.
Carry me in your wallet,
far afield to Thailand
or just down the pub
where we would meet.
Exchange pleasantries in parks
or laugh over lunch,
for I am woven into your great
battle tapestry forevermore.

WOLFHEART

Come now, children.
There is no time to cry,
for Wolfheart is a warrior
and warriors never die.
They soldier on through fire.
They grit their teeth 'midst all the pain.
They let you know it was for you
with the final drop inside their veins.

No, Wolfheart was a soldier,
and he'd remind you every day.
Although his light was fading,
he would never, ever say,
for Wolfheart gave that Wolfheart smile,
much wider than the rest.
That simple smile distracted from
that bomb within his chest.

So, when they lay him down to rest
among the kings and queens and lovers,
place one hand across your breast
and the other in your brother's.
Let the sound fade from the world.
Let the landscape drain of colour.
Feel that rhythm in your chest,
for Wolfheart still beats on like thunder.

III

WHAT IS LOVE?

WHAT IS LOVE?

I will not buy you diamond ring.
I will not send you roses.
I will not stand with you for pics;
I will not hold for poses.
I will not thank you for your help.
I will not kiss you slowly.
I will not hold your hand in streets.
I will not worship you as holy.
I will not pen you birthday cards;
I will not send you gifts.
I will, however, lay you down
And spread my love across your tits.

SIZE 11

Often, when I'm down
and I hate the day ahead,
I think to myself,
"Hell, at least I'm not the guy
who has to put the little bundles
of rolled up paper into
the ends of trainers at Sports Direct."

But he probably has
a working perception of love,
so I guess maybe it's a tie.

FOR YOU

For you,
my dear obsession of the week,
I would toil through wind and fire
until my legs were weak.

Okay, well, maybe not wind and fire.
Wind, maybe,
but definitely not the fire part.
There's no way I wouldn't burn my feet,
and what use would that be
to you or me?

Now that I think about it,
I wouldn't do the wind bit, either.
It'd probably knock me on my arse,
or at least be quite uncomfortable.

~

Lemme think about this for a minute.
I would walk over some Lego for you
at most—
but not any of the sharp pieces,
like the crystals,
or one of those pieces
with the studs on each side,
which are properly sharp.
No, I would walk on Lego for you,
obviously.
Just a few of the 2x4 bricks—
you know, like the classic Lego brick.
The one they use in all their advertising.
I would walk on some of those
for you.

~

Maybe a long one too.

~

For you,
sweet and delicate summer echo,
I would walk gently
upon a few pieces
of well-placed Lego.

PROCESSING

I write you poems
where your name
boils down to "you"
because writing you
into a poem
is easier
than apologising.

UNTITLED POEM #12

I only ask that you kiss me softly,
for my lips have yet to heal.
Impart gently, for mine are cracked,
though yearn for yours to feel.

TATTOO

You're under my skin
and inside of my mind.
I can't scrub you off,
try as I might.

A monochrome scar
from the time I was young—
it hurt for a while,
but now I'm just numb
to the way that it was
before you were in
part of my life,
part of my skin.

UNTITLED POEM #13

It's hard to find the words to fix
what words themselves have split,
and when the words are world to me,
I swallow, scratching grit.
I witness what my words have done
and live through what they heal,
but mind it wanders onto yours.
A rupture they shan't seal.

My words, they begged you, do not cry.
And simply wilted, like a clover,
you recoiled as if bit by snake
while I mulled the words thereover.
Alas, my words escaped me fast,
not with intent to kill,
and though destroying worlds with them,
I said them ever still.

With words in air and fist-grasped hair,
I left you there to linger,
locks shutting hard and leaving car,
never to feel it under finger.

COOKING FOR ONE

1. Return second bowl to cupboard.
2. Retrieve dirty knife from back.
3. Rinse blade and cut open packet.
4. Repeat step 3.
5. Realise you've done it again.
6. Ready water to boil.
7. Reluctantly place both blocks into water.
8. Remember the way she liked it.
9. Disregard step 8. Do it the way you like it.
10. Remove noodles from water.
11. Retreat to bedroom.
12. Remain there all day.

~

Serves ~~two~~ one

UNTITLED POEM #14

I am a coward in your arms
but out of them too.
While the world is asleep,
I awaken with you.

PEACHES AND TULIPS

It is in dimpled cheeks
and flaxen hair,
in toast and berries,
a relaxing pear,
a fruit plucked from the tree
that grows from me,
on the branch that you
will never see.

It is in peaches and tulips
on cold summer nights,
pastel and cream.
You painted them right
in the cracks and the holes
of my quivering brain,
secure in the fact
that we both were the same.

It is in coffee and caramel,
macchiatos and shortbread,
in cafe cup foam.
The smell lingers in my head
while you tactfully roam
your fingers across
the gaps in my teeth.
Where once I was lost,
you brush up with ease
removing the plaque
and replacing with seeds

from the berries you placed
in the glass of mint julep.
I'm remembering you
amidst the peaches and tulips.

HOMECOMING

Shotgun wedding in Toulouse, France—
step on the floor if you're willing to dance
with me, the boy in his scuffed blue
jeans with a hole in his heart shaped like you.

Rest your head on my shoulder
while my hand taints your waist.
Your skin on mine,
you start to smoulder.
I crave your lips for just a taste
of a life I've always wanted to live.

Let me take you to the prom
forty years ago,
when my hair was black
and just before
I'd lost my back,

to slow dance with you
no more.

I promised you then,
and I promise you now
that you were mine.
No matter how
the times would change
and the people too,
I'd still be here
to dance with you.

ANXIOUS

Not a single word rhymes with "anxious."
The best I can offer is "blanket,"
like the one I lie under all day,
wishing all the anxious away.
So, I put in my headphones
and light up a candle.
We'll turn off our hormones
(they're too much to handle).
Let's settle in for hours.
Let's do it again.
This evening is ours
to cry and watch *FRIENDS*.

UNTITLED POEM #15

I have found a peace
in our restlessness;
a joy in the knowledge
that outside this room,
nothing else matters;
that you
and I
are all there is.

VERMISSE

I talk to a sleeping grenade.
I drop my keys in the mud,
wiped them off with both of
my eyes.
They're drawn to
an empty space on a sofa
which a black stain used to grace,
and I hear nothing back.
Vermisse, vermisse, vermisse.
But I tell him of all the stars
that were out last night,
pointing to each one
he would have loved
and equally each one
he would have howled at,
the greatest of them all.
I tell him of the stars
that I would pluck,
like twinkling fruit
to crush into juice,
or a salve

to smear on his heart
so that tomorrow he could
remember how to bark.

∽

Did you know that eighty percent of the ocean is unexplored?
I know.
Despite your best efforts.
but this part was yours,
you know it in its entirety.
You know this place;
not a stone
or shell
or wave could displace you.
Tell me
why you went to the sky
when the sea was so close,
waiting for you…
As I am, at the beach.
I have come here
only twice without you,
trying to hear your noise,
the ticking in your chest
over the crest
of a thousand unsplit waves.

ASHES

Brush off the ashes from my lapel,
angel of the breaking day.
Replace them with fingerprints
or words we cannot say.

SONNET OF THE LONELY MAN

Your palm in mine, it feels a summer dream.
Soft, gliding skin shall smooth my every touch.
A steady hand, you are my daily crutch.
My love, my life, you're more than you might seem.
You gift me change, so sweet as clotted cream.
On finger fourth, a ring I wish to clutch.
Surely, that one can't say it's too much?
Just I, and "Girl from TESCO's Retail Team."
And though she knows me not by any name,
our love is pure; I swear it all the same,
for man and wife of twenty years been wed
will rarely share their touch in lover's bed.
And though I leave the shop today, I'll see
my love in every morn at eight-thirty.

UNTITLED POEM #16

Wake up
to morning dew,
unbrushed teeth, last night's clothes,
the safety of your outstretched arms—
to you.

GHERKIN

My love for you
is contained in a thin slice
of pickled cucumber
plucked from the top of a Big Mac.

Do not cast aside
the flaws you wish to fetter.
Press thine gherkin 'pon mine tongue,
for its taste is all the better.

ONE MORE DAY

My only wish
is that you held on
just one more day.

One more day
for me to let you off the leash,
to watch you run
up those great white stairs
to a new,
painless life.

UNTITLED POEM #17

This was the fifteenth blank page
I have devoted to you today,
And as of yet,
the only one unsullied
by my inability to capture what I want to say.

There are thousands of words
mingling in my mind,
joining in brief parlance
before they decide
to evaporate at the tip of my quill.

Leave me
to wonder
if I ever truly will
discover the rare combination,

that virgin sentence,
to commit to ink
to bare your name.

Those eyes flay the beast
that I shall never tame.

UNTITLED POEM #18

I will love you
'til I'm purple
in the lip
and eye,
'til you tell me
to stop,
'til my hands
are wrenched
from your sides.
I will love you
until I cease
to know
who you
are or
who
I am.

∽

Or until I drag myself

out of the hole
we dug ourselves.

IV

SILVER LININGS

JANUARY 6TH

This morning, I couldn't stop
bouncing my leg and sweating,
and I didn't get up
to take my pill
for over an hour,
so that was pretty rough.

But according to ONS,
roughly 1,817 people were born
on average today in the UK.
So, I guess there's 1,817 silver linings
to the cloud over my head.

Happy birthday!

UNTITLED POEM #19

Oh, child, I only wish I were a plastic bottle,
empty.
So, discarded,
you might kick me across the street.

A RAT I MET IN A SOUTHAMPTON PARK

The stories do not befit you, rat,
harbinger of disease,
plaything of cat.
Sure, you once brought with you plague,
but that was far from yesterday.
In fact, you are much sweeter now.
Shed the black;
a coat of brown
is how you stand before me, rat.
But there is precious little time for that,
for, rat, our time was only brief.
That running man,
a chronal thief.
Why did you flee? He meant no harm.
Spare robbing me of playful charm.
I'd question why you're terrified,
but now I think I've realised
the reason you were so surprised
was that I was in your house,
not mine.

UNTITLED POEM #20

There is a visceral
and indescribable happiness
contained in your clutch,
a soft reconciliation
and a kiss on the forehead,
a promise that it is over now
and brighter days are ahead.

A LITTLE RHYME FOR OUR LORD AND SAVIOUR

Nakey cat,
nakey cat,
oh, how I wish to wake to that.
Skin on show,
no hair can grow.
Oh, Bingus is that cat, I know.

Nakey cat,
nakey cat,
oh, he wears a little snapback hat.
Bingus boy,
bingus boy,
oh, there's no hope. He must destroy.

HAPPINESS IS AN UNBUILT LEGO SET

Happiness is an unbuilt Lego set
reclining in the shadows of the wardrobe
behind the board games that
haven't been played for years.

O, plastic paradise,
ye unsullied maiden,
like the fresh and supple
summer blueberry,
thou art a choking hazard
if under the age of three.

OATS

I can't feed the ducks
without a twenty-minute buffer
to furiously Google,
"Bread safe for ducks?"
"Feed ducks legal UK?"
"BREAD MAKE DUCKS SICK?"

Usually, I miss my chance
to feed the ducks
before I have to go home
with a loaf of stale bread
and a tub full of oats.

I just want to feed the ducks.

UNTITLED POEM #21

There's a sock in my drawer
that I really should throw out
'cause if a smell could make a noise,
then this sock would shout.
There's an exercise in passing time
contained within the cotton.
The only reason it's still here
is because I've honestly forgotten
to peel it from the wooden drawer
and to place it in the bin.
If the devil himself would smell it,
he would name me king of sin
because it's harder than rock
and it stands up on its own.
So, place a crown on my head
and place me upon my throne.

DANCING RATS

I wander through dimly lit parks,
dancing with the rats
that plague our city streets,
going over numbers,
stepping on my feet
to avoid jiving on this pest.
I decide it better to simply stamp
my own bone to mush
than to crush
the cousin mouse outside my house,
whose colours never run
when the sea meets the sun
on the shore, I'm sure.
They're waiting there for me—
little rats dressed in hats,
ball gowns, and tapping flats.
It's such a shame
their little canes
get caught
in metal traps.

~

But I brush past butts
of cigarettes and stuff
I couldn't even name.
It's tough to argue that
the rat, with sharpened teeth
and fur coat black,
shouldn't get the chance to tap
under stars and skies of black
when the people are at home.
They bemoan the rat attacks—
shredding bin bags of black,
tiling kitchen floors with tat
and refuse and food
and a tasty midnight snack
to fuel another ratty lark
while the people rule the park.
In the day, the people play
and leave their mark across the park—
the very treats that they forbade
the rats to take away
from their tatty refuse sack.
And when night takes over day,
and the people fade away
to their homes with walls of grey,
there's a rapture on the greens
of scenes you've never seen,
of rats in ecstasy
weaving 'tween my feet.
Each one beholds a treat:
a scrap of donner meat—
nay—a chip, or crisp, or fry, or
choccy chunk, or little lump
of sugar from a child.
Some mild feast between my feet.

The fancy rats begin to eat
at the ball to end them all
while the sun is in the East,
for when she rises in the West,
they go back to work again.
Groups of ten descend
on the houses of the men
with the best weekly shop,
the fops who get it dropped
off by Ocado, or Sainsburys
or Lidl at a push.
But for now, they rest their heads
on the poison in the bush.

WORM

Worm
Wormy, wriggly little thing.
Wormy, little wriggly thing.
Fleshy, wobbly, wormy ring
around the rosies.
The wibbly, jiggly, wriggly roses.
A-tishoo, a-tishoo.
We all feed the worms.

SWIMMING POOL

Swimming pool,
swimming pool,
oh, take me to the swimming pool
with no lifeguard or bombing rule.
Oh, take me to the swimming pool.

Swim with me.
Swim with me.
Oh, splash me in that saltless sea.
It's mostly pee, so it's not clean.
The owner can't afford chlorine.

Swim around.
Swim around.
Oh, take me where the fun is found.
The wave machine that's underground
is out of bounds since Steven drowned.

~

Swimming session,
swimming session.
Oh, you needn't have had swimming lessons.
Who is Steven? Don't ask questions.
I swear it's just an urban legend.

~

Swimming day.
Swimming day.
Oh, take me to the swimming place.
The door is shut; they locked the gate.
Police want to investigate.

~

Swimming pool.
Swimming pool.
Oh, they closed down the swimming pool.
We had assembly at our school.
They said the owner of the pool—
a man, they said—was awfully cruel.
He's been threatened now with legal action
for "health and safety procedures that were, frankly, not up to
satisfaction."

~

Swimming pool,
swimming pool.
Oh, how I'll miss the swimming pool.
Though Steven now is but a ghoul,
at least we got the day off school.

UNTITLED POEM #22

Stop to breathe
the air the Earth
wants to gift you.

It may be your last
for a while.

COME BACK TO THIS

"Come back to this,"
I write, knowing full well
this page'll never see the light
of day again as long as I live,
for looking at it fills me with
a regret and a wish
that'd I'd given the time
to finish my thoughts,
to conclude my rhyme,
to sum up my ramblings,
to close what I'd penned,
to have found the strength
to give you your—

(Come back to this.)

THE END